Sibylline

BY
MARC VINCENZ

with illustrations by
Dennis Paul Williams

AMPERSAND BOOKS

AMPERSAND BOOKS
www.ampersand-books.com

ISBN: 978-0-9861370-6-8

Cover and back cover design by Marc Vincenz
Cover art: *Blond Leaves*, 2008, Dennis Paul Williams
Interior design by F.J. Bergmann

List of Illustrations

Table of Contents

I. The Mermaid & The Monkey

II. The Infant & The Stinging Nettle

Sibylline

By
Marc Vincenz

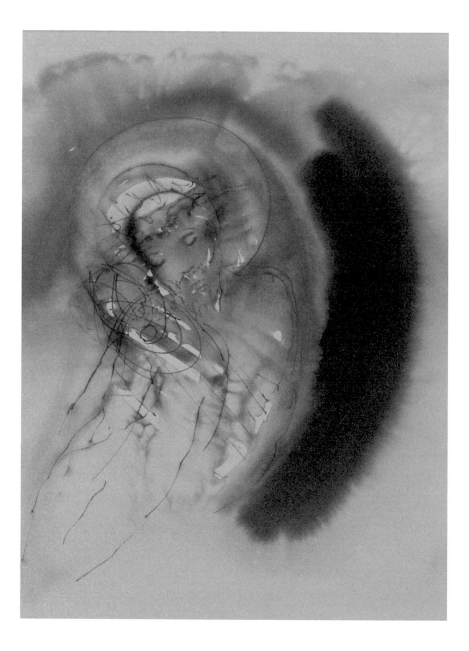

Not odd that what's on my mind,
when expressed, comes out weird, jumbled. Don't berate;
no gun with its barrel screwy can shoot straight.
    Giovanni, come agitate
for my pride, my poor dead art! I don't belong!
Who's a painter? Me? No way! They've got me wrong.

—from *The Complete Poems of Michelangelo*
(trans. John Frederick Nims)

I.

The Mermaid & The Monkey

i. An unsurpassed rule of thumb:

Opposable.
Approachable.
A parable.

Unprecedented.
Percentages.
Patronage is a political strategy.

Perspective revolutionizes everything we see.
It touches the skies

& casts its shadow over distances,
over the humors of a city.

In the next great commission
it's the taste that matters—

glorifying the original sins
of the *maestro della bottega.*

& the birth of Venus,
Botticelli's pagan mythologies—

to stop the devil dancing
on his shoulders,

that master of misogyny.

ii. & to measure the light in all things,

to see Daniel in the lion's den,
serene rather than heroic

(in motion)
& the projection of human form
on heaven's body,

just as Apollo became Jesus
& the blue light
in an Attic August surpasses

the details of posture &
the colonnades & the columns &—

a natural selection of forms feeding

on the spiritual crises,
on the human,
on the heroic,
on the divine,

from within the vault of dark ages
that follow the Fall

& into the hands of dictatorships,
despotisms or democracies

& other magical words that rattle
in the spiritual comfort of relics,

in the concrete substance
that civilizes—

where the true nature
of a building

is forgone space.

& the dreaming magi
in the vaults' echoes

in the love's labors of citizens

giving way to the splendor

of the city giving way
to the flocking pilgrims

or the "effects of good governance"

that surpass
the Black Death

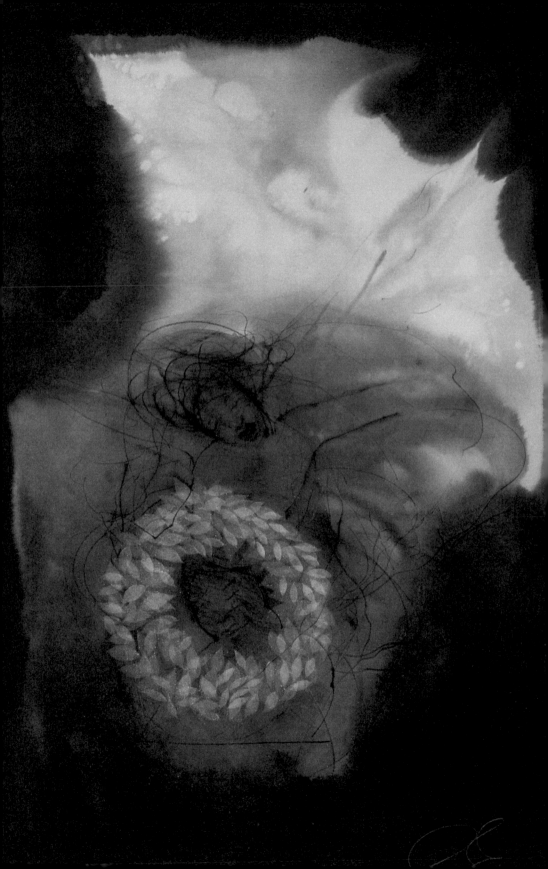

iii. & the greatest city of Rome in decay in a day,

the outpouring
where Death itself

becomes a public theater—
in suspension …

Where God made man
because he loved to hear stories—

Christ's agonies for woman & man
in a time when there was no divorce

& the scales of Archangel Michael glimmer gold

as armies march on
to bombard city walls,

& then that falling
upon Aladdin's den
as Christ upon his cave

& the four horsemen
rhapsodic,

tantalized by tortoiseshell
& rhino-horn & quetzal-feather

as surmised in Dürer's *Ritter, Tod und Teufel*—

melancholy on the dark side of genius

& that last word.

The Teutonic torture—
the twisted hands of the Virgin;

O, the therapy of music
in the Atomic Age

& the torment & trial in the wilderness
the wild fantasies of Grünewald.

Was Aztec gold
a vision of the future?

iv. & in the Pantheon where Rafael was buried,

The Transfiguration,

a measured symmetry
of high society, unfinished.

The Last Supper, a ghost.
compelling, yet

lascivious, licentious
&—elusive.

In completion, reduction
or transfiguration.

The dichotomy of Apollonian or Dionysian principles.

& then, the self-doubt
of an artist with a heroic ambition.

& from that Goliath of marble
the small block of David
from the very skin of the stone,

an evocation
to impress
all comers.

Watch!

As Plato points
toward heaven
Aristotle points
toward the dirt.

& as God touches the finger of Adam,
so Adam touches the hand of another—

so tantalizingly tender
that spiral upon spiral

in the spirit
of the index finger.

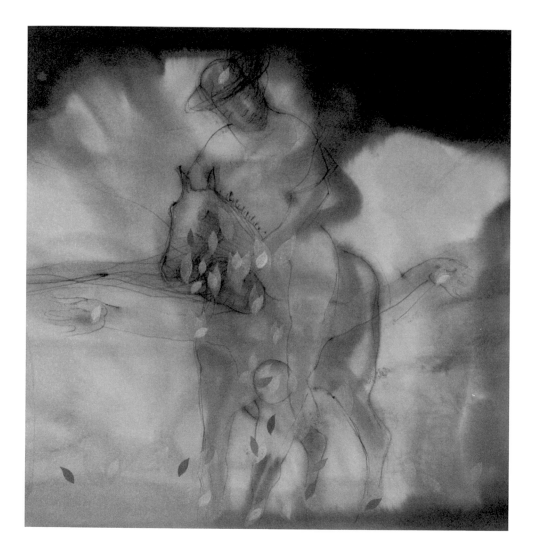

*v. & all this unity, wisdom, wealth, & an ideal
projection*

The illusion of two canopies.

Surely there's more to this canonization lark?

Even when Mercury, our god of money,
gives the party an elevated status

among the doctors & the magi,

how to remain
        at the center
                of power

& rework
        the word
                of love?

vi. *Loft & air*

No brush, no chisel
lightens the soul.

To work through stone,
to find the wall of love

& the ice—
the wall of ice

now dissolves
in unison

with the industry of men,
rhetoric, theater & illusion—

to dramatize yourself
as an ideal man,

rich in trade & craft
& so to come to some fortuitous conclusion

behind the mask
of democracy

in this Pantheon of small gods,
& the desire

to impress

Minerva,
        Mercury,
                Apollo.

Unique in the world
of ever-blooming myrtle.

vii. Light through glass in the Annunciation

YHWH.

The lion, the divine love.

Spaces of unpredicted clarity;
the turbulent light
that emerges
through the darkness.

Across the altar

                in the mass
as the glory

                of angels
suffuses in light.

& in the down-glow,
dogs play
just enough

to convince us
to believe.

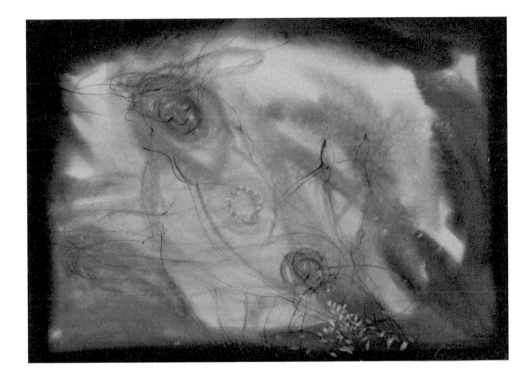

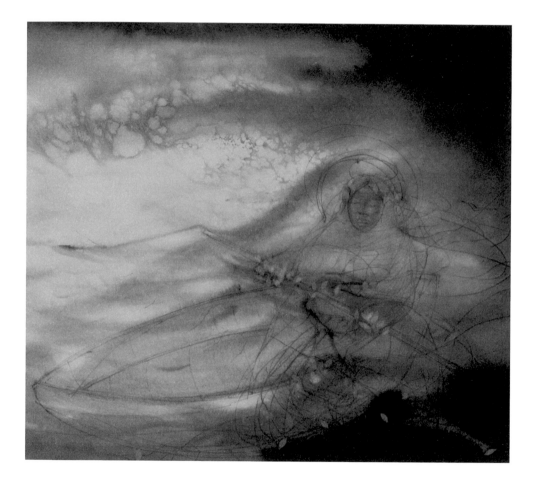

II.

The Infant & The Stinging Nettle

i. Counterrevolution

The seeing & adorning,
& where the mind will be
taken care of,

in the harmony
of the spaces
loved in, lived in.

From this place
the water services

the kitchens, the gardens
& the most excellent fruit.

This painting is large
& could hold

many many
figurines.

ii. The eyes that behold

in the fountain of the aristocrat's garden
among the swans & ducks,
& goldfish,
the king of the beasts
brandishes a sword—

& once again
the light resounds
divine providence

& the bees carry
the keys to the kingdom.

Is it not a time
to draw perspective?

iii. The heartbeat of a building

Transverberation.

Fragrant hymns of praise
& divine celebration—
the smoke of creation.

Journeys that do not end.

Surpassing the sweetness of pain,
the institution's divine right to rule.

What is the vocabulary of power?

You can't read the features
until you're up close to the travails,
observe the naked benevolence,

the descent from the cross
with only one hand
on the reins—

O the arcs & the swirls …

Where the eye cannot focus
as one myth assails another

& suffused with nostalgia
within the shadows
of sculpted space,

in the everyman
of everyday
departing for the Isle of Cythera.

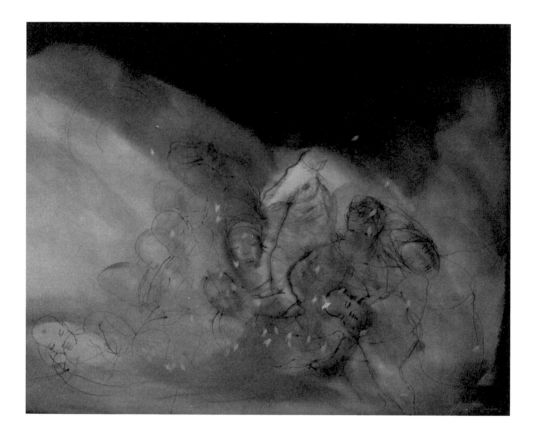

iv. & in the microcosm of the garden,

The effects of past time,
the truth unveiled,

movements
between the hills & the dales.

        ✦ ✦ ✦

The art of liberty.

The staking out of order
& that fever
of Revolution.

Was it just the failure
of the harvest?

or was it the oath
in the mausoleum?

v. *A secular* pied d'etat, *a political ideal*

Now the stars of the empire

    far from the bean

        of enlightenment,

the urban proletariat

    & the clouds of revolution

        gathering.

The abstraction

    that prepares us

        to give our lives.

The anecdotal.

    A natural being

        with untamed appetite.

The primacy

of the eye

on the surface of appearances

An imprecise definition of form.

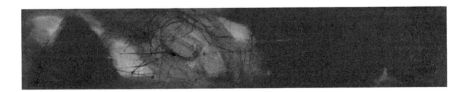

Oh how the light

    modifies matter

        & toys with grand design.

vi. Worshipping the serene Buddha

When does the disquiet
become bourgeois

& the yawning background

descend

      in celestial revelations?

vii. *On the Sun's consciousness*

How to handle the modern?
How to find a kiss
for the whole world?

Behind a beautiful curtain
the objects of mystery & desire.

The dislocation.

& the savage made assailable through—

impromptu, flimsy,

but deadly serious
pure plastic rhythm.

    ✦ ✦ ✦

Oh to follow the flight of the swallow
through the storm of the future

& to become
that bird
in space
in your own right.

viii. *How to remove the object from the center of the eye?*

Space & sense

            & the dream

& then, the enthusiasm

of Man as iceberg.

All those babblers, dilettantes & swindlers

opening doors

into different futures,

following the minotaur.

ix. *But a shadow falls upon history*

repairing the shattered cultures
& thus
backs
turn

into their own expression
followed by sand

& waste

& rubble,

O—no subject,
but content …

no document
seared
in the corners

of a lifetime
within a fixed timeline
degrading the colors—

the speed of change,

    the saturation

        of objects,
            packing,

preparing

    for a wide spread—

unheroic,

anywhere,

anything,

no more windows,
but a field, a horizon,
an assemblage,
a tremulous clutter

in the small,

the mundane,

the profane, then the real

x. & the disposable,

A libation.
A liberation.

The transformation of the flesh,
sweeping away,
generating a vision
of what already is

with immediate
content—the dissidents
& their images of glory.

Watch closely!

   ✦ ✦ ✦

Here come the corporate collectors.

Abstractions have become ordinary
& the myth of progress
grinds down to a tiretrack.

What controversy?

xi. Where's the leverage in the pluralism?

What then can we say
of the symbols of belief?

Can you hear the silence
of history breaking?

The phantoms inform
but do not transform.

Inject yourself back
into the earth
& become a sphere.

Become evidence
of former lives.

You can only predict
the probability
at odds
with experience.

xii. Still, in the knot of perspective,

A voiceover says:

All roads are traveled.
Vibration determines everything.

O, if only
for a quick, tight
Hollywood
ending.

Acknowledgements

Excerpts and previous versions of "Sibylline" appeared in *Plume Poetry* online and *Plume Interviews Vol. 1*. Many thanks to editor Daniel Lawless, and to Nancy Mitchell for her insightful interview.

About the Artist

DENNIS PAUL WILLIAMS is a person of immense and radiant energy.... the world Dennis Paul Williams lives in is immediately recognizable. Also recognizable is the truth of transcendence.

Williams' imagination is fueled by the sacred feminine. In these paintings, it is that sacred feminine figure that is dominant. She may be a Madonna, she may be a sacred feminine vessel of some ancient tribe, and she may be a powerful antique goddess leading a people. But she may be too one of his daughters, his wife Paulette, or his mother, or his grandmother, the latter especially influential in shaping Williams' view of himself as a person.

The music he loved as a child, and which provides part of his work "for a living," is all over his vast works. His spiritual energy spins like dervsishes in his imagery. His paintings are fields in which his daughters reside. His wife is there; his uncle, brothers, father, grandmother—all personages he reveres. So are horses and fish. The lowly chicken is there. Birds and angels and rabbits are there, too. And so are the old prophets—all drawn from a rich imagining of the ancestral icons on whose shoulders Dennis Paul Williams so lovingly and so brilliantly stands.

Williams' paintings are conversations with the reverential and the divine; with what has passed, and what is coming toward us with the terrible swiftness and certainty of unquestioning love.

—Dr. Darrell Bourque

About the Author

MARC VINCENZ is British-Swiss and the author of nine poetry books. *New Pages* called his last collection, *Becoming the Sound of Bees* (Ampersand Books, 2015), "… a book where doors can fly off in 'butterflies of rust,' where poems can stretch themselves sideways across the page, and worlds can build upon themselves in dizzying descriptions. This is a collection for those who enjoy digging their claws into strange landscapes and getting pulled forth by a culmination of sounds."

Vincenz is also the translator of many German-language poets, including Herman Hesse Prize winner Klaus Merz, Werner Lutz, Erika Burkart, Alexander Xaver Gwerder, Andreas Neeser, Robert Walser and Jürg Amman. His translation of Klaus Merz's collection *Unexpected Development* was a finalist for the 2015 Cliff Becker Book Translation Prize and will be published by White Pine Press in 2018. He has received several grants from the Swiss Arts Council and a fellowship from the Literarisches Colloquium Berlin. His own work has been translated into German, Russian, Romanian, French, Icelandic, Georgian and Chinese; Bucharest's Tractus Arte Press released a Romanian translation of his collection *The Propaganda Factory* at the 2015 Bucharest Book Fair.

Although he has lived and traveled all over the word, Marc Vincenz now resides, writes, translates and edits in western Massachusetts.